Cover design by Mike Zafiropoulos, Zafro Creative, LLC, www.zafrocreative.com

Marketing by Ashley Peterson, https://www.behindthebusinessconsulting.com/books

Edited by Kate Meadows, Kate Meadows Writing & Editing Services, LLC, www.katemeadows.com

ISBN: 9798323838097

www.donniejoseph.com/books

5 SIMPLE STEPS

TO FINANCIAL ORDER

DONNIE JOSEPH

ADDITIONAL BOOKS
BY DONNIE JOSEPH

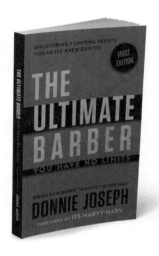

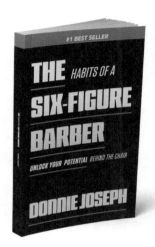

Scan the QR code below to access a complete collection of my other books and learn more about me.

WWW.DONNIEJOSEPH.COM/BOOKS

EFFORTLESS BOOKKEEPING FOR BARBERS

WHY EASYTRACK™?

- ✓ YOU'RE NOT TRACKING INCOME AND EXPENSE
- ✓ MAKES TAX SEASON A BREEZE
- ✓ HELPS MAXIMIZE WRITE-OFFS
- ✓ EXTREMELY AFFORDABLE
- ✓ ENTITY SETUP

EASYTRACK
BOOKKEEPING

LEARN MORE

MONEY LIKES SPEED™

WWW.THEEASYTRACK.COM
ADMIN@THEEASYTRACK.COM

Table of Contents

Foreword

By **Kale Goodman**, co-founder of Easier Accounting and *The Real Business Owners* podcast

S**TARTING A BUSINESS** is HARD AF!

Good thing if it doesn't work you can just write it all off on your taxes, right?

Wrong!!!

Tax code actually says everything you spend to get up and running is considered "start-up cost" and the majority of the start-up cost has to be amortized over 15 years.

So, for the purposes of math, if you spend $25k to get up and running, you can only write off $1,666 a year for the next 15 years.

That sucks when you're self-funding a new hustle.

However, as soon as you are considered "OPEN FOR BUSINESS," you can start deducting the full cost of running your business.

For any barbers that are getting into business or starting another one, let me help you:

Becoming, "OPEN FOR BUSINESS" can actually happen pretty quick and easy, depending on what your business does.

Take the example of a cool coffee trailer business I recently launched called, Grit + Grind.

If I set up my LLC, grab my business license, set up a business bank account, get a merchant account (to accept credit cards) and order my first batch of products, I can sell to my first few customers from a wagon and an ice chest in the street for under a couple thousand bucks.

That's not what I'm doing in this business, but the point is this:

Once you CAN make your first sale, you're considered "OPEN FOR BUSINESS" and can start writing off a whole lot more immediately.

So, before you spend money on a fancy website, business cards, barber tools and equipment, or spend more than you need to up front, try to think of a way you can be "open for business" right away.

If barbering is just one of the services you provide under your brand, what are some other services you can provide that can get your brand open for business?

For example, consulting. Anyone can be "open for business" by charging for what they know.

Maybe you know how to create really cool barber-related content, or maybe you know how a barber can get more clients into his shop.

Still unclear on how you can be open for business? Make a social post that you're "now accepting new clients" and offer a payment method through which people can pay you.

"Open for business" means that you're pursuing profits and that you can start making your first sales.

Do this before you go crazy spending a ton of money.

I share this little gem with you barbers so you can actually write off as many expenses and lower your taxable income right away.

Starting a business doesn't have to be hard AF. This is why I love this book that Donnie wrote for you. He breaks down the first five steps of creating a legitimate business so you can utilize the tax code to your greatest advantage.

Put this book to use right away. You won't regret it!

Introduction

ALRIGHT BARBERS, it's time to address a dirty little secret in our industry — one that I've been guilty of, you're likely guilty of, your coworker may be guilty of, and even the shop owner where you work might be guilty of. It's the secret of mismanaging our finances.

While there are a select few who might grasp the principles I've laid out in this book, most of us haven't. It's not because we don't want to. It's because we don't know how to, and we don't know where to turn. Well, your search ends here, because I've penned this book for you. The *5 Simple Steps to Financial Order*, is a blueprint for you to follow to get your finances on track once and for all.

To help you avoid the financial struggles and pitfalls so many barbers experience, I'm going to walk you through how these struggles show up and how you can get past them. Let's be honest: we are in an industry that glamorizes the quality of our work but fails to offer encouragement or insight into properly managing the finances required to make a name for ourselves.

But it doesn't have to be that way. This book offers a simple, step-by-step guide to help you organize your finances effortlessly. If you've been grappling with money management issues — mixing haircut earnings with personal funds, neglecting to track your income and expenses, falling behind on taxes — don't feel ashamed; you're not alone. In fact, you should be proud of yourself for taking the initiative to read this book, because it indicates that you recognize the problem and that you're determined to change your circumstances.

When it comes to financial mismanagement, there are two types of people who struggle: those who don't know what to do and those who know what to do but fail to act. I'm willing to bet you fall into the former category, but that changes today.

Unlike my other books, which delve into thought-provoking narratives, this book gets straight to the point, offering practical advice that you can digest in just 20 minutes and start to implement immediately.

If you learn nothing else from reading this book, remember this: MONEY LIKES SPEED™. If your actions are impeding its flow — whether coming in or going out — you're not in sync with money. Money likes to circulate. The faster you facilitate its movement and organize it in a way that allows it to move in and out efficiently, the more it will flow toward you in abundance!

Here's to your future financial success,

Donnie Joseph

WHERE DO YOU STACK UP
AS A BARBER?

Take our quick online assessment to uncover the areas where you excel or where you need improvement.

SCAN ME TO TAKE THE TEST

Screenshot your score and share results with me @donnie.joseph

WWW.THEBARBERTEST.COM

STEP 1:

Establish an Entity and Employer Identification Number

WELCOME to the first and most important step of your financial journey as a barber! As you embark on the path of entrepreneurship, establishing the right foundation for your business is paramount to your long-term success in business. Establishing a solid financial foundation is similar to creating a proper guide at the beginning of your haircut to ensure a successful haircut.

In this chapter, I'm going to walk you through how to establish yourself as a business entity and how to get an employer identification number. There are multiple types of business entities. So that you can decide which entity is best for you, I'll break down the most common: the Sole Proprietorship, the Limited Liability Company (or LLC), the S-Corp, and the C-Corp.

1

UNDERSTANDING THE IMPORTANCE OF THE FIRST STEP

Setting up the proper business entity lays the groundwork for your entire business venture. It determines how you and your business will operate, how you'll be taxed, and most importantly, how your personal assets will be protected. Unfortunately, many barbers overlook and/or underestimate the importance of this initial step, leading to unnecessary stresses and potentially disastrous consequences down the road.

UNDERSTANDING THE DIFFERENT BUSINESS ENTITIES

As a barber, starting out on your own as an independent contractor is essentially starting your own business. You might work independently (as a 1099 contractor) at someone else's business, you might rent a suite, or you might be starting your own barber shop. My question for you is, how protected are you and your assets? The answer depends on the business entity you set up. Let's break down the options:

Sole Proprietorship: This is the simplest form of business ownership. If you're cutting hair on your own, without any partners or employees, you're automatically considered a sole proprietor. A sole proprietorship is easy to set up and manage. But keep in mind that you're also personally responsible, meaning that you could be held legally liable for any debts or liabilities your business incurs. That would require you to use your own money or assets to cover those costs.

Limited Liability Company (LLC): An LLC offers more protection for your personal assets than a sole proprietorship, because your personal assets are separated from your business liabilities. This means that if you are working on the general public and your barber business faces legal trouble or debt, your personal assets (like your car or home) are safe. An LLC is relatively simple to form and doesn't require as much paperwork as a corporation.

S Corporation (S Corp) and C Corporation (C Corp): These are more complex business structures that are generally more common with larger companies. They offer liability protection like an LLC but involve more administrative tasks and have different tax implications. As a small barber business, you'll likely find an LLC to be the most suitable option.

BENEFITS OF FORMING AN LLC

Now, let's talk about why forming an LLC is a great choice for your barber business:

Limited Liability: By forming an LLC, barbers create a legal barrier between their personal assets and business liabilities. This means that in the event of a lawsuit or debt, personal assets like savings, homes, and vehicles are shielded from creditors.

Flexibility: LLCs offer flexibility in management and ownership structure. You can choose to manage the business yourself or appoint managers, and you can have one owner (single-member LLC) or multiple owners (multi-member LLC).

Tax Advantages: LLCs offer flexibility, allowing barbers to choose how they want to be taxed. By default, LLCs are pass-through entities, meaning profits and losses flow through to the owners' personal tax returns. This often results in potential tax savings compared to corporate taxation.

Professionalism and Credibility: Operating as an LLC demonstrates a level of professionalism and credibility to the barber business. It shows clients, suppliers, landlords and potential partners that you're serious about your profession and committed to operating ethically and responsibly.

Selling Your Business: An LLC offers a distinct advantage when it comes to selling your business. Unlike a sole proprietorship, where the business is essentially an extension of the owner, an LLC has its own legal existence separate from its owner(s). This means that when you sell your barber shop, you're not just transferring ownership of a business; you're transferring ownership of a legal entity with its own assets, liabilities, and operating agreements.

EXAMPLES OF LLC NAMES

Choosing the right name for your LLC is important, as it represents your brand and identity. Here are some examples to inspire you:

Fresh Cuts Barber Co., LLC
Sharp Styles Studio, LLC
Cuts & Shaves, LLC
SLT Enterprises, LLC
Faded Barbershop, LLC

Keep in mind that if you plan to expand into other businesses such as developing your own product line, a barbershop, or barber training videos, you may want to create a more general LLC name such as the above example from one of our clients, SLT Enterprises, LLC. A name like SLT Enterprises, LLC, allows the owner to branch out and create a secondary business name (or multiple business names) underneath the LLC by choosing a DBA ("doing business as") option. As this company expands, it can add on multiple DBAs. Generally, an LLC can register and operate multiple DBAs to conduct different lines of business or to market various products and/or services under different names.

If you do not plan to expand into other businesses, it's fine to stick to a more specific name. For example,a name such as Faded Barbershop, LLC, will most likely only ever be a barbershop.

When choosing a name, there is no right or wrong answer. There is only what is right for you and your business goals.

ADVANCED

Let me preface this entire section by encouraging you to consult with your accountant to obtain recommendations tailored to your individual circumstances. Their advice will be more accurate to your business needs.

WHEN AN LLC MAY NOT BE THE BEST CHOICE

While forming an LLC offers numerous benefits for many barber businesses, there are certain situations where it may not be the optimal choice. Here are some scenarios where alternative options, such as structuring your LLC as an S-Corp for tax purposes, could be more advantageous:

Tax Optimization for Moderate Income: If your taxable income falls within the range of $35,000 to $60,000 after accounting for deductions and write-offs, there's a tax strategy worth considering: electing S-Corp taxation for your LLC. By doing this, you can potentially reduce your self-employment tax burden and optimize your overall tax liability.

Existing LLCs and Tax Planning: If you already own one or multiple LLCs and seek to implement advanced tax strategies, converting an LLC to be taxed as an S-Corp could offer additional benefits. This approach allows you to leverage the advantages of S-Corp taxation, such as minimizing self-employment taxes and optimizing distributions, while maintaining the limited liability protection afforded by the LLC structure.

TAX BENEFITS OF AN LLC TAXED AS AN S CORP

When you elect S-Corp taxation for your LLC, you unlock a range of tax benefits that can significantly impact your bottom line. Here are some key advantages:

Reduced Self-Employment Taxes: As a sole proprietor or traditional LLC owner, you're subject to self-employment taxes on all business profits. By structuring your LLC as an S-Corp, you can potentially reduce these taxes by taking a portion of your income as a distribution thereby lowering the portion subject to self-employment tax.

Tax Savings on Distributions: Unlike sole proprietors and traditional LLC owners, S-Corp shareholders can receive distributions of profits that are not subject to self-employment taxes. This allows you to optimize your income mix, potentially lowering your overall tax liability while still accessing the funds you need for personal expenses.

Flexible Compensation Structure: With an S-Corp, you have the flexibility to structure your compensation in a more tax-efficient manner. While you must pay yourself a fair and reasonable salary for your position, you can allocate additional profits as distributions, which are not subject to payroll taxes. For example, as a barber you could pay yourself $34,000 per year as a W2 employee. Any remaining money you make in business underneath your S Corp is taxed at a 15% lower rate. There are multiple ways of utilizing your S-Corp and payment structure(s), some of which will depend on whether you have only one or multiple LLCs. The main idea is that you want to maximize tax efficiency while ensuring compliance with applicable regulations so you can retain more of your earnings for reinvestment or other financial goals

Potential Qualified Business Income Deduction (QBID): Under certain circumstances, S-Corp shareholders may be eligible for the QBID, a deduction introduced by the Tax Cuts and Jobs Act. This deduction can provide further tax savings for qualifying business income, potentially reducing your taxable income and overall tax liability.

While an LLC is a popular choice for many barber businesses due to its simplicity and liability protection, it may not always be the most tax-efficient option, especially for individuals with moderate incomes or those seeking advanced tax planning strategies. By considering the option of electing S-Corp taxation for your LLC, you can potentially optimize your tax situation and maximize your financial success as a barber business owner.

IMPORTANCE OF ESTABLISHING AN EMPLOYMENT IDENTIFICATION NUMBER (EIN)

Now that you have your entity established, let's discuss the significance of obtaining an EIN for your barber business:

Separate Identity: An EIN, also known as a Federal Tax Identification Number, gives your business its own identity for tax purposes. It's like a social security number for your business.

Business Banking: With an EIN, you can open a business bank account separate from your personal account. This will make it easier later when it is time to manage your finances and keep track of business expenses.

Credit Establishment: Having an EIN allows you to establish credit in your business's name. This means you can apply for business credit cards and loans, helping you access funding to grow your barber shop.

Hiring Employees: If you plan to expand and hire employees in the future, you'll need an EIN for payroll purposes. The EIN simplifies the process of reporting taxes and ensures compliance with employment laws. Side note: "Employees" can also include a spouse or children. This option can be a useful tax strategy when you are earning enough income that you want to hire members of your family to work for you.

COMMON MISTAKES BARBERS MAKE

Failure to Protect Personal Assets: Without the shield of a proper business entity like an LLC, barbers risk exposing their personal assets to business liabilities. In the event of a lawsuit or financial hardship, creditors could go after not only the business assets but also the barber's personal savings, home, and other possessions.

Tax Pitfalls: Operating as a sole proprietorship might seem convenient at first, but it often results in missed opportunities for tax savings. Many barbers are unaware of the potential tax benefits offered by entities like LLCs, which can lead to paying more taxes than necessary.

Limited Growth Opportunities: Operating without the proper business structure can hinder your ability to expand and grow your barber business. Without the flexibility and scalability provided by entities like LLCs, barbers may find themselves struggling to attract investors, secure financing or hire additional barbers.

Difficulty in Separating Business and Personal Finances: Mixing business and personal finances, also known as *commingling*, is a recipe for disaster. It is the most common error I see barbers making. If this is you, it is extremely important that you follow the steps in this book IMMEDIATELY and get on the right track. If you need help, please visit our website, www.theeasytrack.com, or email us at admin@theeasytrack.com. Every day that goes by is a day you are putting yourself at risk and ultimately losing out on potential savings. Without a distinct separation between personal and business finances, tracking expenses, managing cash flow, and preparing your taxes becomes nearly impossible. This lack of financial organization can lead to inefficiencies and errors that impede your barber ability to thrive.

IN SUMMARY

Forming an LLC and obtaining an EIN are crucial steps in establishing a strong financial foundation for your barber business. They provide protection, flexibility and opportunities for growth, setting you on the path to financial success. By avoiding common pitfalls and making informed decisions, you'll pave the way for a thriving barber business. So, take the leap and lay the groundwork now. You won't regret it.

IN SUMMARY

STEP 2:

Open a Business Checking Account

CONGRATULATIONS on completing Step 1 of your financial journey as a barber! Now that you have your business entity established and your Employer Identification Number (EIN) in hand, you're ready to take the next step: opening a business checking account.

WHY OPENING A BUSINESS CHECKING ACCOUNT IS IMPORTANT

Think of your business checking account as the heartbeat of your barber business. This account is where you track all the money that's coming in and going out of your business. A business checking account is important for several reasons:

Separation of Finances: Opening a business checking account allows you to keep your personal and business finances separate.

This separation is important for maintaining accurate records, tracking business expenses apart from personal expenses and simplifying tax preparation.

Professionalism and Credibility: A dedicated business checking account demonstrates professionalism to your clients, suppliers, landlords and partners. It adds credibility to your business and instills trust in potential customers, showing that you're serious about your barbering profession.

Legal Compliance: Operating with a separate business account ensures compliance with legal and regulatory requirements. It helps maintain the integrity of your business entity and protects your limited liability status, especially if you've formed an LLC.

WHY TIMING MATTERS

Now, you might wonder why we're discussing opening a business checking account after establishing your LLC and obtaining an EIN. The reason is simple yet important:

Account Transitioning: If you were to open a business checking account first as a sole proprietor and then later form an LLC and obtain an EIN, you'd likely need to close the existing account and open a new one in the name of your LLC. This process can be time-consuming and may lead to confusion or disruptions in your banking operations.

By waiting until after you've established your LLC and obtained your EIN, you ensure that your business checking account is set up correctly from the start, saving you time, effort, and potential headaches down the road. Learn from my mistakes — it's better to do it right the first time.

CHOOSING THE RIGHT BANK

When selecting a bank for your business checking account, there are a few factors to consider. You'll want to know a bank's fees and charges, what types of online banking features are offered and the bank's track record for customer service.

Fees and Charges: Look for a bank that offers competitive fees and minimal charges, especially for small businesses like yours. Is there a minimum balance requirement? Are there transaction limits? Is there a cost to notarize documents, print business checks or receive monthly bank statements?

Online Banking Features: Opt for a bank that provides convenient online banking services, including mobile banking apps and digital payment options. This feature can streamline your business activities and make running your business more convenient.

Accessibility: Choose a bank with convenient branch locations and ATMs to ensure easy access to your funds.

Customer Service: Prioritize banks with excellent customer service and support, as you may need assistance with account-related queries or issues.

PERSONAL RECOMMENDATION

Relationships are vital to your success as a barber. That's why my favorite option for a barber's business banking is a local credit union. I've found that local credit unions tend to be more friendly and understanding toward barbers and their businesses. Credit unions often offer personalized service, community-focused values and a genuine interest in supporting local entrepreneurs like yourself.

Local credit unions may also provide additional benefits such as lower fees, competitive interest rates and flexible lending options tailored to small businesses. Plus, by banking with a credit union, you're contributing to the growth and prosperity of your local community, building stronger connections and partnerships along the way.

IN SUMMARY

Opening a business checking account is a critical step to establishing the financial infrastructure for your barber business. By separating your personal and business finances and choosing the right bank, you set yourself up for success and ensure smooth operations moving forward. Remember, with each step you take, you're one step closer to achieving your financial goals as a successful barber entrepreneur.

STEP 3:

Get a Business
Credit Card

WELCOME to Step 3 of your financial journey as a barber, getting a business credit card. In this chapter, we'll explore the importance of utilizing business credit, building your business credit profile and reaping the benefits of earning points or cash back rewards. Plus, I'll share my number-one choice for a business credit card.

WHY UTILIZING BUSINESS CREDIT IS IMPORTANT

Business credit plays a vital role in the financial health and growth of your barber business. Here's why it's essential to leverage business credit:

Separation of Personal and Business Finances: Just as we emphasized the importance of separating personal and business finances with a dedicated business checking account, a business credit card further solidifies this distinction. Using a business credit card for business expenses helps maintain clear financial boundaries and simplifies record-keeping for tax purposes.

Building a Business Credit Profile: Just like individuals have personal credit scores, businesses have credit profiles that lenders use to assess that business's creditworthiness. By responsibly using a business credit card and making timely payments, you can establish a positive credit history for your barber business. This can prove invaluable when seeking financing or negotiating favorable terms with suppliers and vendors. Keep in mind that having access to extra capital can also provide benefits to you if you want to work with bigger clipper companies or need to buy in bulk.

Earning Points or Cash Back Rewards: One of the most enticing benefits of using a business credit card is the opportunity to earn rewards on your spending. Whether it's cash back, travel points or other perks, these rewards can provide savings and incentives for your business. It's like earning bonuses for expenses you would incur anyway.

ADDRESSING BAD PERSONAL CREDIT

If you have bad personal credit, it may be necessary to pause Step 3 and address your credit issues. Here are some tips for repairing your personal credit:

Dispute Old Debts: Request removal of any outdated or inaccurate negative items on your credit report, especially debts over seven years old. A simple letter to the credit bureaus requesting removal may suffice. If you go this route, send your letter by certified mail with, "return receipt requested." This will give you a timestamp and verification that your document was received. The credit bureaus have 30 days to investigate and correct any inaccurate information on your report.

Credit Building Strategies: Consider strategies to improve your credit score, such as becoming an authorized user on a trusted individual's credit card or working with a reputable credit repair company like 60-Day Credit Repair. You can learn more at www.60daycreditrepair.com. I don't receive any sort of commission for sharing this resource with you, but I know the owners and they are good guys. So if you do visit their website and use their services, make sure to tell them I sent you.

Avoid Debt Consolidation Scams: Be wary of companies offering to consolidate your debts, as these may lead to further financial challenges and exacerbate your credit issues.

Once your credit is repaired, you can resume Step 3 and proceed with obtaining a business credit card to support your barber business's financial needs. Remember, responsible credit card use is key to building and maintaining a strong financial foundation for your business's success. A credit card is not a free pass to buy whatever you want.

APPLYING FOR A BUSINESS CREDIT CARD

When applying for a business credit card, follow these steps:

Research Card Options: Explore various business credit card offerings to find one that aligns with your business needs and preferences. Consider factors such as rewards, fees, interest rates and benefits.

Apply Online or In Person: Complete the credit card application either online or in person, providing accurate information about your business and financials.

Income and Spending Estimates: Provide realistic estimates when it comes to your business's income and projected spending on the credit card. For new businesses, you may need to estimate based on your business plan or expected revenue.

Wait for Approval: Once you've submitted your application, await the creditor's decision. Approval timelines vary, but you should receive a response within a few business days, if not immediately.

MY PERSONAL RECOMMENDATION FOR A BUSINESS CREDIT CARD

As a barber and business owner, choosing the right business credit card is crucial. I recommend American Express, and here's why:

Great Customer Service: American Express is renowned for its exceptional customer service. Whether you have questions about your account, need assistance with a transaction or require support for a dispute, their customer service team prompt and personalized assistance.

Multiple Credit Card Options: American Express offers a diverse range of business credit cards to suit various needs and preferences. From cash back cards to travel rewards cards, there's an option for every type of business. For new businesses like yours, the AMEX Blue Cash Preferred is particularly appealing, for reasons I explain below.

0% Introductory Rate: One of the standout features of the AMEX Blue Cash Preferred (at the time of writing this book) is its 0% introductory rate for 12-18 months. This allows you to carry a balance on your card for 12-18 months without incurring interest charges, providing financial flexibility as you navigate the early stages of building your barber business. Just remember to pay off the balance before the introductory rate expires to avoid accruing interest on unpaid balances.

No Reporting to Personal Credit: Unlike some other business credit cards, American Express business cards typically do not tie to your personal credit report. This means that any balances or activity on your business credit card won't impact your personal credit score. This separation can be advantageous, especially if you need to carry a balance for business purposes.

THE IMPORTANCE OF USING ONE CREDIT CARD FOR BOOKKEEPING:

It might be tempting to get multiple business credit cards as you're starting your business, especially if you have multiple credit cards for personal use. But I suggest you maintain a single business credit card to start with. Along with significantly streamlining your bookkeeping process, here are some other reasons why using a single business credit card is a good idea:

Simplified Tracking: With all business expenses consolidated on one credit card statement, tracking and categorizing expenses becomes much more manageable. This simplifies your bookkeeping tasks, reduces the risk of overlooking transactions, and ensures accurate financial records.

Easier Reconciliation: When it's time to reconcile your accounts, having just one credit card to review simplifies the process for both you and your accountant or bookkeeper. There's less room for error, and it saves time and effort compared to reconciling multiple credit card accounts.

THE IMPACT ON ACCOUNTING COSTS

As your business grows and your needs evolve, you may find yourself considering additional business credit cards. However, it's essential to weigh the potential impact on accounting costs. Here's why:

Increased Complexity: Managing multiple credit card accounts introduces complexity to your accounting processes. Each account requires reconciliation, monitoring, and oversight, which can add to the workload for your accountant or bookkeeper.

Higher Fees: Many accountants and bookkeepers charge based on the complexity of your financial records. Having multiple credit card accounts may result in higher fees due to the increased time and effort required to manage and reconcile those accounts.

BEING RESPONSIBLE WITH YOUR CREDIT CARD:

Responsible credit card use is paramount to your financial success and stability. What does it mean to be responsible with your business credit card?

Paying Balances in Full: Aim to pay off your credit card balances in full each month to avoid accruing interest charges. This practice not only saves you money; it also demonstrates financial discipline and reliability to creditors. Some business owners choose to take advantage of the 0% introductory interest rate while building their business and intentionally carry a balance on their cards with the intention of paying their entire balance in full just before the 0% interest rate expires. Please avoid this strategy if you are inexperienced or not generating the necessary revenue to pay off your entire balance.

Monitoring Spending: Keep a close eye on your credit card spending, ensuring that your spending aligns with your budget and business priorities. Avoid unnecessary or frivolous purchases, and prioritize essential business expenses.

Managing Credit Limits: Be mindful of your credit limits and avoid maxing out your credit card. Maxing out your credit card makes it harder to dig yourself out of debt and makes it harder to receive business loans from lenders. You could also be overextending your finances, when more is going out than coming in. When you utilize credit responsibly, you keep your credit utilization ratio within manageable levels.

IN SUMMARY

Getting a business credit card is a pivotal step in establishing and managing your barber business's finances. By leveraging business credit, earning rewards and choosing the right credit card, such as the AMEX Blue Cash Preferred, you can unlock valuable benefits and streamline your financial operations. Remember to use your credit card responsibly, pay off balances in full whenever possible and capitalize on the perks and rewards to maximize your business's success. With each swipe of your business credit card, you're not just making purchases; you're leveraging someone else's money to run your business while you can keep your hard-earned dollars.

STEP 4:

Track Your Business Income and Expenses

CONGRATULATIONS on making it to Step 4. In this chapter, we'll explore the importance of diligent record-keeping, provide examples of what tracking income and expenses entails for a barber, discuss the benefits of staying financially organized and dive into some basics of proper book-keeping. We'll also highlight how the first three steps of the *5 Simple Steps to Financial Order* have prepared you for this pivotal stage of financial management.

For barbers, tracking income and expenses can be one of the most overlooked tasks. While we excel at making money through our craft, we often struggle with organizing and managing the financial aftermath. This struggle can lead to a host of problems down the road, from tax headaches to cash flow problems.

IMPORTANCE OF TRACKING INCOME AND EXPENSES

For a barber running their own business, tracking income and expenses is paramount. Here's why:

Financial Awareness: Tracking income and expenses provides insight into your business's financial health. It allows you to monitor cash flow, identify trends and make informed decisions about budgeting and spending.

Tax Compliance: Proper record-keeping helps to ensure compliance with tax obligations. By accurately documenting income and deductible expenses, you can minimize tax liabilities and maximize deductions, ultimately saving money come tax time.

Business Performance Evaluation: Regularly tracking income and expenses enables you to evaluate your business's performance over time. You can assess profitability, identify areas for improvement and set realistic financial goals based on historical data.

Legal Compliance: Maintaining organized financial records is essential for regulatory compliance and legal protection. It provides documentation in case of audits, disputes or inquiries from regulatory authorities.

WHAT TRACKING INCOME AND EXPENSES LOOKS LIKE

For a barber, tracking income and expenses involves several key tasks. Here they are:

Recording Daily Sales: Keep a log of daily sales transactions, including the services rendered and corresponding revenue. This could be done electronically using accounting software or manually in a ledger or spreadsheet.

Documenting Business Expenses: Record all business-related expenses, such as rent for your barber shop, supplies, equipment purchases, utilities, marketing costs and professional fees. Be diligent in categorizing expenses to ensure accurate reporting. As a side-note, I keep 3 separate gallon size ziplock bags handy — one at my office, one in my vehicle and one at home. All of my paper receipts go into those bags, and later get consolidated and filed. It's not a fancy system, but it works for me. I'm also old school, so if my method doesn't work for you, the more modern option is to download a tracking app and scan your receipts right into the app.

Separating Personal and Business Transactions: Maintain separate accounts for personal and business finances to avoid commingling funds. Use your business checking account and credit card exclusively for business expenses.

Tracking Cash Flow: Monitor cash flow regularly to ensure sufficient funds for operational expenses and identify any cash shortages or surpluses. This helps with continued budgeting and financial planning.

BASICS OF PROPER BOOKKEEPING

Proper bookkeeping involves several key principles and practices, which I'll explain here. If it sounds like an alien language to you, don't be alarmed! I felt the same way when I was first introduced to it. If this sort of thing excites you, then dive right in. If it doesn't, then don't worry about it, because, as you'll see in Chapter 5, you don't need to fully understand it.

Accrual vs. Cash Basis Accounting: Understand the difference between accrual and cash basis accounting. Accrual accounting recognizes revenue and expenses when they are incurred, regardless of when cash changes hands, while cash basis accounting records transactions only when cash is received or paid. More than likely, as a barber you'll be using cash basis accounting.

Double-Entry Accounting: Adopt the double-entry accounting method, which ensures that every transaction has equal and opposite effects on both sides of the accounting equation (assets = liabilities + equity). This helps maintain accurate and balanced financial records.

Chart of Accounts: Develop a chart of accounts, which is a structured list of all accounts used by a business to classify financial transactions. This includes assets, liabilities, equity, revenue and expenses, organized into categories for easy reference.

Reconciliation: Regularly reconcile your accounts, comparing financial records against bank statements to identify any discrepancies or errors. This helps ensure accuracy and integrity in your financial reporting.

BUILDING ON PREVIOUS STEPS

The first three steps of the *5 Simple Steps to Financial Order* have laid a solid foundation for effective income and expense tracking:

Establishing Entity and EIN (Step 1): By forming a legal entity and obtaining an Employer Identification Number (EIN), you've created the framework for conducting business transactions and separating personal and business finances.

Opening a Business Checking Account (Step 2): Opening a dedicated business checking account provides a centralized platform for managing financial transactions and facilitates the tracking of income and expenses.

Getting a Business Credit Card (Step 3): Utilizing a business credit card further streamlines expense tracking and offers additional benefits such as rewards and financial flexibility, enhancing your ability to monitor and manage cash flow.

By following these steps sequentially, you've equipped yourself with the necessary tools and infrastructure to effectively track income and expenses, setting the stage for proper financial management and business success. Now that you know what to do, we need to discuss *how* to actually do all this. That's where Step 5 comes in.

IN SUMMARY

Tracking income and expenses is a critical aspect of running a successful barber business. By maintaining accurate records, adhering to proper bookkeeping practices, and leveraging the foundation established in the previous steps of the *5 Simple Steps to Financial Order*, you'll gain valuable insights into your business's financial performance and ensure compliance with tax and regulatory requirements. Essentially, you'll be operating as a professional barber and business owner.

STEP 5:

Hire a Bookkeeper

YOU MADE IT to Step 5 of the *5 Simple Steps to Financial Order*! Now that you have a general understanding of how to properly put your finances in order for your barber business, it's time to hire a bookkeeper. In this chapter, we'll discuss the benefits of enlisting a professional to manage your financial records, discuss key considerations when seeking a bookkeeper and explore the transformative power of delegating tasks to focus on your strengths.

First, I'd like to commend you for making it this far in the book. It says a lot about you, where you are and more importantly where you are going! The question you have to ask yourself now is, "Do I want to go there alone?" or "Do I want to do what other successful businesses do and go with the help and expertise of others?"

> *"If you want to go fast, go alone.*
> *If you want to go far, go together."*
> —Unknown

THE POWER OF DELEGATION

As barbers, we often pride ourselves on our ability to multitask and handle various aspects of our business. To say it plainly, that's a big part of why we've gotten as far as we have in life, because we've done it alone, without the help of others. That works to a certain point. But even the best hustler can only hustle so much before they cap themselves out. I've learned this first hand, trying to scale my businesses over the years. Trying to do it all can lead to overwhelm, inefficiency and ultimately, burnout. That's where delegation comes in.

Imagine this: You're behind the barber chair, providing exceptional service to your clients, honing your craft, building meaningful connections and making money. Meanwhile, behind the scenes, your bookkeeper is tracking your income and expenses, ensuring financial accuracy and compliance and simply organizing your money in a way that, more than likely, is better than you can do yourself. By delegating financial tasks to a professional, you free up your time and mental bandwidth to focus on what you ARE good at — cutting hair, providing excellent customer service to your clients and growing your business.

BENEFITS OF HIRING A BOOKKEEPER

Now, let's explore the tangible benefits of hiring a bookkeeper:

Expertise and Accuracy: A proficient bookkeeper possesses specialized knowledge and skills in financial management. They accurately record transactions, reconcile accounts, and prepare financial statements, ensuring the integrity and accuracy of your financial records.

Time-Saving: Delegating financial tasks to a bookkeeper saves you precious time that can be reinvested into your core business activities. Instead of struggling with spreadsheets and receipts, you can focus on serving your clients, growing your business, pursuing your passion and spending time doing things you actually enjoy doing.

Financial Insight: A professional bookkeeper can provide valuable insights into your business's financial health and performance. By analyzing financial data and trends, a bookkeeper can identify opportunities for cost savings, revenue growth and strategic decision-making.

Peace of Mind: With a trusted bookkeeper managing your financial affairs, you gain peace of mind knowing that your finances are in capable hands. This alleviates stress and allows you to approach your work with clarity, confidence and excitement.

WHAT TO LOOK FOR IN A BOOKKEEPER

When selecting a bookkeeper, consider the following criteria:

Communication and Compatibility: Choose a bookkeeper who communicates effectively, understands your business goals and aligns with your working style. Clear communication and rapport are crucial for a productive and harmonious working relationship.

Technology Proficiency: Ensure that your bookkeeper is proficient in using accounting software and technology platforms relevant to your business. Familiarity with industry-standard tools streamlines workflow and enhances efficiency.

Trustworthiness and Integrity: Trust is the foundation of any successful partnership. Seek references, testimonials or referrals to assess a bookkeeper's reputation, reliability and ethical standards.

THE PATH TO GROWTH

Ultimately, hiring a bookkeeper is not just about managing numbers — it's about embracing a mindset of growth and empowerment. By recognizing your strengths and delegating financial tasks to a professional, you're creating space for innovation, creativity and personal fulfillment.

In the journey of entrepreneurship as a barber, success is not measured solely by financial metrics but by the quality of life, fulfillment and impact we create. By investing in professional support and leveraging the strengths of others, you're not only strengthening your business; you're also nurturing your own well-being and growth.

As you embark on this transformative step of hiring a bookkeeper, remember: it's not just about balancing the books — it's about balancing your life in a way that ensures a successful future, not only as a barber and business owner, but also so that you can enjoy your life and the lifestyle you've created.

PARTNER WITH ME AND EASYTRACK™ BOOKKEEPING

Now, if you're serious about getting your finances in order, committed to being a good person, and promise to help other barbers (like you) in the future, then you are the type of person I want to partner with. Just like when building your clientele in the barbershop you want to work with clients you enjoy being around, we feel the same way about building our clientele at EASYTRACK™ Bookkeeping. If that resonates with you and you feel like we can help you get on the right track with your finances, I urge you to partner with my company, a company built specifically to help barbers like you manage your business finances so that you can do more of what you're good at — being a barber. To do so, simply visit our website, www.theasytrack.com, or email us at admin@theeasytrack.com.

EASYTRACK™ Bookkeeping not only provides professional bookkeeping services, but we can also help you with **Step 1: Establish an Entity and Employer Identification Number** through our *Premium Barber Starter Pack*. To learn more about this service please visit our website (provided in the last paragraph). Perhaps most importantly, we also share your values of integrity and community support.

That being said, if you choose not to use us, we still value your entrepreneurial journey and are committed to providing you with valuable information. By reading this book, we hope you gained insight into the steps you should take as a business professional.

Remember, whether you choose EASYTRACK™ Bookkeeping or another bookkeeping service, the most important thing you can do is to take proactive steps toward managing your finances effectively and fostering the growth of your barbering business.

With Gratitude,

Donnie Joseph

—————— **IMPORTANT** ——————

New Federal Reporting Requirement for Beneficial Ownership Information (BOI)

UNDERSTANDING BOI AND ITS ORIGIN

Let's start with the basics: Beneficial Ownership Information Reporting, or BOI for short, is all about being transparent about who really owns or controls your business. This law, known as the Corporate Transparency Act, was introduced to shed light on the ownership structure of businesses and prevent illicit activities like money laundering and terrorism financing.

WHO IS REQUIRED TO REPORT

Entities that are required to report their BOI include most corporations, limited liability companies (LLCs) and other similar entities formed under state law in the United States. However, certain types of businesses are exempt from BOI reporting requirements, such as publicly traded companies, certain financial institutions, nonprofits and entities with more than 20 full-time employees, among others. It's important for business owners to carefully review the regulations and consult legal advice to determine whether they fall under the reporting obligations or exemptions.

WHY BOI COMPLIANCE IS ESSENTIAL

Here's the important part: if you don't follow the BOI rules, it could end up costing you big time. We're talking about fines of $500-per-day, up to $10,000, and up to two years in prison, if you don't provide the required information on time. In other words, make sure you comply with this new requirement.

KNOW YOUR DEADLINES

Here are the deadlines you need to keep in mind:

- If your company was created or registered before January 1, 2024, you have until January 1, 2025, to file your BOI.

- If your company was created or registered in 2024, you have 90 days to file your BOI.

- If your company is created or registered on or after January 1, 2025, you have 30 days to file your BOI.

KEEPING THINGS UP-TO-DATE

After you've filed your BOI, you will need to update it if there are any changes or corrections to the beneficial ownership information you've already filed. This ensures that FinCEN (Financial Crimes Enforcement Network, with the U.S. Treasury Department) always has the most accurate and current information about your business.

WHERE TO GET HELP

You can find guidance materials and additional information by visiting www.fincen.gov/boi. This website offers resources to help you navigate the BOI process and make sure you're on the right track. And remember, while it's free to file by yourself, if you currently have an LLC or other entity and need help filing your BOI, EASY-TRACK™ can help you. So, don't hesitate to reach out if you need support.

Note: If you use my company, EASYTRACK™ Bookkeeping, to form your LLC, we will automatically file your initial BOI as part of our *Premium Barber Starter Pack.* To learn more about this service please visit our website, www.theasytrack.com.

About the Author

DONNIE JOSEPH was a barber working behind the chair for nearly 15 years before he became an entrepreneur focused on creating six-figure incomes for barbers.

But his journey isn't just one of success. Joseph has had to overcome many challenges that stemmed from the difficult environment in which he was raised. Joseph's life is a testament to the fact that your environment doesn't always dictate your future. Take it from him: becoming great is a choice, and anyone can become great if they are willing to do the work.

Today, Joseph is a family man, entrepreneur, multi-business owner, author, mentor and member of the elite Real Business Owners Mastermind group. He has a passion for community outreach and encouraging others. In his 20-plus-year career, Joseph has achieved financial success in the barber industry and has been influential in progressing the barber profession.

His impact extends further with the establishment of EASY-TRACK™ Bookkeeping, a specialized company dedicated to assisting barbers in managing their finances effectively.

He strives to inspire others who want to unlock their potential behind the chair so they can also have a greater impact on the world around them, making their corner of the world a better place.

THERE ARE 2 TYPES OF BARBERS

WHEN IT COMES TO MANAGING FINANCES

1

THOSE *WHO DON'T KNOW* WHAT TO DO

2

THOSE *WHO KNOW* BUT FAIL TO ACT

ARE YOU NUMBER ONE?
WE WILL HELP YOU.

EASYTRACK
BOOKKEEPING

WHERE DO YOU STACK UP
AS A BARBER?

Take our quick online assessment to uncover the areas where you excel or where you need improvement.

SCAN ME TO TAKE THE TEST

Screenshot your score and share results with me @donnie.joseph

WWW.THEBARBERTEST.COM

ADDITIONAL BOOKS
BY DONNIE JOSEPH

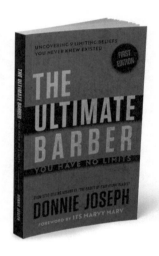

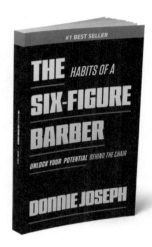

Scan the QR code below to access a complete collection of my other books and learn more about me.

WWW.DONNIEJOSEPH.COM/BOOKS

Made in the USA
Columbia, SC
11 August 2024

40343633R00041